Tomie dePaola's
CHRISTMAS TREE
BOOK

CHRISTMAS
TREE
FARM

CUT YOUR OWN

Tomie dePaola's
CHRISTMAS TREE BOOK

HOLIDAY HOUSE · NEW YORK

Special thanks to Jack Santino, professor at Bowling Green
State University, for his expert review of the text

Originally published as *The Family Christmas Tree Book*
Copyright © 1980 by Tomie dePaola
All Rights Reserved
Design by Semadar Megged
HOLIDAY HOUSE is registered in the U.S. Patent and Trademark Office.
Printed and bound in June 2022 at Toppan Leefung, DongGuan, China.
www.holidayhouse.com
Second edition hardcover published in September 2019
Second edition paperback published in October 2021
3 5 7 9 10 8 6 4

Library of Congress Cataloging-in-Publication Data

dePaola, Thomas Anthony. The family Christmas tree book.
SUMMARY: A family discusses the origin of the Christmas tree as it decorates its own.
1. Christmas trees—Juvenile literature. [1. Christmas trees. 2. Christmas] I. Title.
GT4989.D46394.2'6828280-12081
ISBN: 0-8234-0416-1 (hardcover) | ISBN: 0-8234-0535-4 (paperback)

ISBN: 978-0-8234-4238-6 (hardcover second edition)
ISBN: 978-0-8234-4992-7 (paperback second edition)

Hey, Mom and Dad, how did Christmas trees get started?

Yeah, who invented the first one?

Well, no one's exactly sure who invented the first one, but decorated trees and branches at Christmastime have been around for a long, long time.

5

In the Middle Ages, December 24th was called Adam and Eve's Day. On that day, a play was put on in front of the churches.

Evergreen branches with apples on them were part of that play. They represented the Tree of Paradise.

I guess people liked the bright green branches, because when the medieval plays were no longer performed, people brought evergreens and even small fir trees into their homes.

Especially in Germany, they put not only apples on the trees, but also paper roses and flat wafers. The apples represented Adam and Eve; the roses, the Virgin Mary; and the wafers, the Christ Child.

These trees were called CHRISTBAUM.

Dad and I just read that in Germany, they had other Christmas things too.

One was called a PYRAMIDE. It was made out of wood and was decorated with branches and candles.

The other was called a LICHTSTOCK, and it was a flat triangle-shaped rack just for candles.

Right. Lots of German people had either a PYRAMIDE or a LICHTSTOCK and a CHRISTBAUM standing side by side in the same room. Finally, the candles were moved from the PYRAMIDE to the tree.

Of course, the old-time trees were small and were put on tables. It wasn't until the Christmas tree came to America that it reached from the floor to the ceiling.

When did Christmas trees come to America?

Well, the first trees known about were decorated in 1747 by a group of people from Germany called Moravians. They lived in Bethlehem, Pennsylvania.

Little by little, as more German people moved to America, there were more Christmas trees. Other people borrowed the custom and by the 1800s many magazines had articles about them.

Famous people had Christmas trees too. In England, Queen Victoria's German husband, Prince Albert, helped to make them popular. He gave decorated trees to schools and army barracks.

And at the palace, there was a separate tree for each of the young princes and princesses.

President Teddy Roosevelt decided not to have a Christmas tree one year, because he was worried that too many trees were being cut down. His son, Archie, was so disappointed that he decorated his own tree and hid it in a closet.

You know, when I was a little girl, we didn't have a Christmas tree stand. Even though they were being made, they were very expensive.

So, my father used to nail wood to the bottom of the tree. Once, we used all of my mother's flatirons to hold the tree up.

But the trees always got very dry, so one Christmas we filled a washtub with coal, put the tree in the middle of it, and added water. I remember we had to pile bricks on top of the coal, so the tree wouldn't fall over.

My mother's rich Aunt Clara had a Christmas tree stand that was a music box. As the music played, the tree went around.

There's a nice legend that a man named Martin Luther was out walking one Christmas Eve, and he saw a fir tree on a hill. It was surrounded by stars.

It looked so beautiful that he decided to surprise his family with a special Christmas tree. So, he put candles on the branches and lit them. The tree looked as though it was filled with stars.

The first electric lights were used in 1882. They were on a tree at the home of Edward Johnson. He was a friend of Thomas Edison, the man who invented the light bulb.

In 1895, Grover Cleveland was the first president to use electric lights on the tree in the White House. Each bulb had to be wired separately on the tree. Strings of lights weren't invented until 1907.

Now, there are all kinds of Christmas tree lights: little ones that glitter like stars, lights that blink on and off, lights that bubble, and even lights that look just like candles.

And here are all our ornaments.

Mom, our teacher told us that once people had to make ALL their own ornaments. They wrapped nuts in pretty paper, used ribbons, cookies, and all kinds of stuff.

We make some of our own ornaments!

Did any of you know that almost all glass ornaments used to come from one village in Germany called LAUSCHA?

They were all made by hand.

American businessmen, including Mr. Woolworth, began importing them and, by 1930, 95% of all glass ornaments hanging on American Christmas trees came from this village.

It wasn't until 1939 that glass ornaments were made in America.

There are so many different ways to decorate a Christmas tree.

The main thing is that every family's Christmas tree is very special to that family.

Ready?

FIGURE A

A MAKE-IT-YOURSELF
ANGEL ORNAMENT

IMPORTANT: Do not cut the decoration from this book.

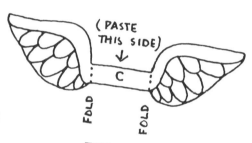

FIGURE B

1. Copy the angel (Figure A) and the wings (Figure B) onto heavy paper.
2. Color the angel any way you wish. Also, color Part A and the front and back of the wings.
3. Carefully cut out the angel and the wings.
4. Fold the "fold-lines" toward the back.
5. Tape or glue Part A on top of Part B.
6. Tape or glue the wings to the angel by matching the C's. Bend the wings.
7. Double a string or heavy thread and push the loop through the hole at the top. Knot the ends together.
8. Hang on your tree.